s'mores

s'mores

Gourmet TREATS for Every Occasion

lisa adams

PHOTOGRAPHS BY JOYCE OUDKERK POOL

Gibbs Smith, Publisher

TO ENRICH AND INSPIRE HUMANKIND

Salt Lake City | Charleston | Santa Fe | Santa Barbara

First Edition

11 10 09 08 07   5 4 3 2 1

Published by

Gibbs Smith, Publisher

P.O. Box 667

Layton, Utah 84041

Orders: 1.800.835.4993

www.gibbs-smith.com

Designed by Dawn DeVries Sokol
Printed and bound in Hong Kong
Specialty marshmallows made by Paul A. Stone of Split Bean Coffee

Library of Congress Cataloging-in-Publication Data
Adams, Lisa.
S'mores : gourmet treats for every occasion / Lisa Adams ; photographs by Joyce Oudkerk Pool. — 1st ed.
    p. cm.
  ISBN-13: 978-1-4236-0091-6
  ISBN-10: 1-4236-0091-6
 1. Cookery (Marshmallow) 2. Desserts. I. Title.

TX799.A33 2007
641.8'53—dc22
                                        2006026578

For my parents, Glen and Cindy,
who shared with me the joy of a campfire

And for John,
my partner in all things

contents

acknowledgments

THIS BOOK WOULD NOT EXIST without the contributions of many, many sweet tooths.

I owe the book's very concept to the Steward family—and the lure of a particularly succulent strawberry on a momentous May night. My many collaborators and taste testers include Glen, Cindy, Dustin, and Katy Adams; Rick, Maria, Leigh Ann, Rhea, and Marina Maze; John, Valerie, Neva, and Bonnie Steward; Carl and Ilima Adams; Tim, Linda, Ryan, Erin, and Patrick McNulty; Art, Renee, Jennifer, Jason, and Rava Frengel; Pat, Terri, Caleb, Travis, Jessica, and Rachel DuBridge; Tom, Mary, Cameron, and Lanie Bruce; Timothy O'Connor Fraser, Tyler Mullins, J. T. Yeh, Warren Madsen, Serena Rundberg, Howard Sweger, Rick Gessner, Melinda Clark, Sean Sanford, Shane Karres, Alicia Irving, Andrew Weiss, Jacqui Stutz, and a handful of hungry kids whose names I never learned (sorry!). I am especially grateful to the very talented Leigh Ann Maze for twice braving the smoke to capture my preliminary s'more photography.

For their eager sampling and fondness for silly recipe names, I must also thank the Superfriends: Erin Lee, Glenda Lee, Vince Novak, Alice Handley, Cory Gowan, Chris Tousseau, Sean Blagsvedt, "Jolly" John Goldie, Colin Daly, and Keith Nicol.

Most of the "hard" work of fine-tuning these recipes happened at home, and so I owe a thousand thanks to John and Emma Heath, who ate whatever I made and endured my endless hours of pondering and tweaking. Never has a family consumed so many s'mores in their own kitchen! With her boundless optimism and brutally honest taste buds, Emma made a fabulous advocate and assistant. And John was there from start to finish, not only tasting and opining but also editing my words and positioning errant marshmallows. I cannot thank him enough for his enthusiasm for this book and his perfect support of me.

This book owes its mouthwatering photos to Joyce Oudkerk Pool and her assistant Sara Jacobs, who captured the true deliciousness of s'mores in every shot.

Finally, I would like to thank my editor Melissa Barlow, and everyone at Gibbs Smith, Publisher, for believing in this book and doing so much to make it the best it could be.

I am indebted to each and every one of you for making this book happen. S'mores would still be boring if it were not for you!

introduction

I've been eating s'mores my whole life, and I have to tell you—they're not very interesting.

Call me a literalist, but it should be nearly impossible to stop eating something called "some more." Yet consistently I found myself brushing s'mores aside to stuff my face with more delectable treats like cake and ice cream and candy.

It didn't seem right. So I set out to invent s'mores that really live up to their name.

In this book you'll find dozens of unbelievably delicious recipes that will change the way you think about s'mores. Using sweets, fruits, and chocolates of every variety, these recipes are designed to embellish the treat we know and love, bringing a little more variety, creativity, and fun to the fire—or to the barbecue, s'more kit, or stovetop. Whether you make s'mores at home or out in nature, I hope these variations make you melt with delight—and reinvigorate your love affair with this venerable dessert sandwich.

what is a s'more?

It's a good question. Until now the definition was pretty obvious: a s'more was a dessert sandwich made from two graham crackers, a piece of chocolate, and a roasted marshmallow. That recipe has been around forever—or at least since 1927, when it was first published in a Girl Scout handbook.

I set out to expand that definition. But as I began to enter uncharted s'more territory, I was left with an unanswered question: What *does* make a s'more a s'more?

After consulting several oracles, I made a decision: while many of the s'more recipes in this book do not contain graham crackers, and a few don't have chocolate, every recipe contains a roasted marshmallow. If you don't like marshmallows, or don't eat gelatin, you can omit the marshmallow from almost all the recipes and still have a delicious dessert (s'mores are flexible that way). But in

expanding the s'more concept, I felt that there had to be at least one common element, one ingredient that linked these recipes to their noble ancestor. The marshmallow, roasted over a campfire, has always been the essence of s'mores—and despite the new recipes and new cooking methods, the marshmallow remains the foundation, and the heart, of this beloved dessert sandwich.

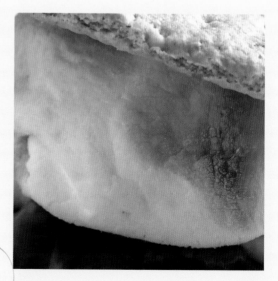

how to make s'mores

It's not just a matter of adding new ingredients. That's a big part of it, of course, but the real key to unbelievable s'mores is melting those ingredients. And that's a step that needs some explaining.

Though we all associate s'mores with campfires, you can make the recipes in this book without exposing even a fingernail to the wilderness. Barbecues, fireplaces, home s'more makers, ovens, and stovetops can deliver the same goods as a stick and a fire pit. So whatever your preferred cooking arrangement, read on to get all the tips and tricks you'll need to make sublime s'mores.

choosing your ingredients

If you're going to make a specific s'more for a specific occasion, well, this one's a no-brainer. Pick your recipe and buy the ingredients. Voilà!

For parties and camping trips, however, I'd highly recommend the Buffet Experience. It can be momentous, even life-changing—especially for those who never dreamed such a thing could exist. Imagine surprising your hardened, unsuspecting campfire cronies with an eye-popping spread of chocolates, sliced fruits, and outrageous toppings, bathed in the flickering light of a propane lantern. Your friends are guaranteed to love you forever and might very well cry with joy.

The best way to plan your buffet is to flip through this book, note the recipes you'd most like to try, and make a list of ingredients. Your budget may dictate how much you buy, but I'd recommend choosing enough ingredients to make at least a few different kinds of s'mores. Be sure to consider the melting factor when purchasing your chocolates—it's very tempting to

save some money by grabbing those giant, thick versions of your favorite candy bars, but keep in mind that if you like melted chocolate—and we will dwell deeply on melted chocolate—you will have difficulty with these monster-size treats. On the other hand, some people prefer their chocolate unmelted, so there's no harm in stocking up on both slender and substantial candy bars when choosing your chocolate.

When it comes to marshmallows, nothing roasts so well as your standard store-bought varieties. In addition to the regular white puff, in some grocery stores you can also find marshmallows coated in toasted coconut (deliciously paired with melted caramel in the Toasted Coconut Caramel recipe on page 96).

However, you can add some beautiful color and interesting flavor to your s'mores by using hand-made marshmallows, now available from many specialty food stores and candy shops (and their websites). These cube-shaped confections feature flavors such as raspberry, banana, and chocolate, and are usually bigger than standard marshmallows. Their shape and size can make them difficult to roast thoroughly, so I like to cut them in half before roasting, or use a metal cooking rod to ensure the centers get gooey. Because these specialty marshmallows can be expensive and hard to find, I have not used them in many of my recipes—but if you have them, feel free to use them in place of regular marshmallows. You will spot several in photos throughout this book. In the Resources section (page 125), you'll also find a list of some places to buy them.

As for graham crackers, use any kind you like. The cinnamon and chocolate varieties taste almost identical to regular honey grahams when used in s'mores, and they do look quite pretty—so you can use them whenever you want a fancier presentation. For an extra bit of chocolate, you can also try topping your s'mores with chocolate-dipped graham crackers instead of plain ones.

you're going to take all that camping?

Folks today have numerous and conflicting ideas about what camping is and should be.

Clearly some campers must still eat nothing but oatmeal and ramen noodles, because after hearing about some of my recipes, a few people have looked at me blankly and asked, "You're going to take all that *camping?*" Well, sure—some of my camping friends eat better around the fire than I do at home! We all believe in eating well in the woods, and that includes great s'mores.

While some of the recipes in this book may be too much for the oatmeal-ramen type of camper, almost everyone should be able to make several s'more varieties using ingredients that they would normally bring on any camping trip. Some of the easiest and tastiest s'mores contain nothing more exotic than fresh or dried fruit. It's also easy to replace plain milk chocolate with your favorite candy bar, or graham crackers with cookies. So don't worry—s'mores are for everyone!

setting up your buffet

Once you're ready to make a night of it, pick a convenient spot and arrange your ingredients. It usually works best to use a well-lighted table a short distance from the fire so that buffet visitors can choose their ingredients without tripping over roasters and sticks. Using a table also keeps the ingredients orderly and out of the grime; you can stash ingredients in different people's laps around the fire, but this lazy arrangement often leads to common s'more afflictions, such as the Unspeakably Broken Grahams, the Suspiciously Vanishing Chocolate Bar, and the dreaded Dirt-Encrusted Marshmallow Bag.

If all this sounds too cumbersome, just make s'mores indoors or during the day. Sure, you'll lose some atmosphere, but you'll also eliminate many of the challenges that can besiege a customary campfire.

cooking your s'mores

One of the biggest and most disappointing lies I've ever heard was that a hot marshmallow will melt a piece of chocolate. This is patently untrue. A hot marshmallow will create a microlayer of warmth between it and a cold, hard chocolate bar, but that's about it. It's a crime, and so I offer a lot of melting tips in this book. While s'mores are still tasty with unmelted chocolate, I believe that the meltiness of a s'more is just as important as its exciting ingredients. So I'll go through the melting techniques for each heat source—fire, barbecue grill, oven, fireplace, s'more kit/stovetop, and microwave—to set you on the course to truly gooey treats.

friendly fire

The best cooking fires are big on coals, not giant flames. You'll have more heat, and at the same time more control, when cooking over coals—and that goes for roasting marshmallows as well as melting chocolate.

The good news is that you don't need a perfect fire to make fantastic s'mores. Most of the fires I use are a mix of flame and coal, flickering in a metal pit with a partially adjustable but not exactly malleable cooking grate. I simply work with what I have, trying to keep the flames and coal-beds apart as much as possible. Then I follow the guidelines below.

If your fire does not have soaring flames, you can place your graham cracker (with chocolate and other ingredients on top) directly on the grate, and simply pluck it off quickly when the ingredients have melted. Obviously, the farther away from the coals, the longer the melting process will take. For this reason I recommend using a bottom graham cracker for most s'mores;

grahams will not fall apart even if stuck on a grill for a long time (though they *will* burn if abandoned for an extended period).

If your fire *does* have soaring flames, you can use a frying pan to melt your ingredients. Put the chocolate-laden graham cracker into the pan, and put the pan on the grate. When the ingredients have melted properly, you can take the pan off the grate and slide the graham onto a plate with a spatula. For best results, do this last step at a decently lit table. If you insist upon doing it around the fire in the dark, have someone else hold your plate so you don't accidentally cast your just-melted delight into the night. Though it can be a bit unwieldy, the pan process can cook several s'mores at once, and it does a good job of melting the ingredients consistently. It also prevents grahams from getting burned. Don't use a fancy pan, though; the bottom can really get scorched.

You can also melt your ingredients by enclosing them in a package of heavy-duty aluminum foil. All you need to do is tear off two same-size pieces of foil (about a foot and a half square should be plenty) and place one directly on top of the other. Lay your graham cracker and ingredients in the middle, and lift up all four sides so that your graham cracker rests at the bottom of the chute. Then roll or pinch the foil together at the top to seal it. (It doesn't have to be pretty.) Set the foil package on the grate or, if you have no flames, close to the coals. Use tongs or a potholder to snatch the foil back, then open it up (it will cool off in just a minute) and slide the s'more onto your plate. This method melts the ingredients well, and is often the best process to use if you are not using a graham cracker for your bottom piece. But grahams and cookies can still burn this way, so don't leave the foil near the coals for too long.

Finally, if you don't want to mess with any extra equipment, you can knife a few gashes into the sides of your uncooked marshmallow and force small pieces of chocolate (chocolate chips work well) inside them. When you roast the marshmallow, the chocolate will melt, and you can then sandwich the whole thing between grahams. The downside? It's difficult to get much chocolate into the marshmallow. Plus, if your marshmallow succumbs to the flames, you lose all the chocolate too! I only use this method with s'more varieties that cannot be melted (such as Black Forest Cupcake on page 86).

Obviously, these melting methods require interaction with hot fires and hot grills, so they should not be attempted by those too young or imprudent to pull them off without getting hurt. While melting the chocolate is more challenging than standard s'more assembly, the extra step—whichever one you choose—will definitely be worth it!

barbecued s'mores

Use your barbecue grill to make heavenly s'mores anytime the mood strikes. The real advantage of s'moring on a grill is that you can use the lid to ensure quick and thorough melting of your ingredients. I don't even roast my marshmallow—I just set it on top of my bottom graham cracker and leave the whole thing under the lid for a few minutes. The marshmallow doesn't turn golden brown, but it does melt over the rest of the ingredients and tastes delicious.

Depending on the kind of grill you have, you may also be able to roast a marshmallow close to the heat while you melt ingredients on the grate. Without a lid, though, your ingredients will take longer to melt, so make sure your graham cracker doesn't burn in the process.

baked s'mores

If you're making s'mores for a large group, the oven is a great way to go. Just grab a baking sheet, line it with foil or parchment paper (if you're an easy-cleanup type), and assemble your s'mores—omitting the top graham cracker (or alternative). Then pop the sheet into a preheated 350-degree oven for 4–6 minutes (oven temperatures vary, so make adjustments as needed). Your marshmallows, while not officially roasted, will puff up and melt over the ingredients; all you need to do, after cooling the s'mores for a minute or two, is add any final toppings.

It's best not to make particularly tall s'mores using this method; marshmallows can melt in unpredictable ways and are liable to plummet off a tower of ingredients. I'd recommend leaving off any fruit or anything else that doesn't need to be melted. Once the cooking is complete, you can squish these ingredients into your melted marshmallow. If you are making a s'more without graham crackers and need to heat both pieces (cookies, for example), just put the top piece next to the rest of the s'more on the baking sheet. Then, when everything is ready to go, complete the sandwich. Whether you're making one signature s'more recipe for all your guests or giving each person free reign over a buffet, the oven method allows everyone to cook and enjoy their s'mores at once.

where the hearth is

S'mores are also fun to make on a wintery evening at home. You probably won't have a cooking grate, but you can use the aluminum foil method (described on page 16) to melt your ingredients while you roast marshmallows over coals or flames.

s'more kits and stovetops

Home s'more-making kits are now available at many specialty stores. These contraptions usually consist of a ceramic burner and tray, outfitted with a grill, metal roasting forks, and a metal pot to hold the fuel.

While these kits are adequate, they present a few challenges to the s'more lover used to working with a real fire. The kits use chafing fuel, which is flammable magenta gel that comes in small tins and burns hot enough to roast marshmallows.

Because the flames burn so hot, you must be very careful with your marshmallow; hold it far from the flame and turn it constantly. Otherwise, the marshmallow will burn, or the skin will turn completely brown before the inside is soft and gooey.

More significantly, the kits are not designed to melt chocolate on graham crackers. The flames will quickly burn any food set on the grill; even aluminum foil is not immune. You *can* place a small frying pan on the grill, however, which will melt your ingredients evenly without burning your graham cracker. The trouble is, you can't melt your ingredients and roast a marshmallow at the same time.

Therefore, my favorite method is two-pronged: I set my s'more kit next to my stovetop. While I melt my toppings on the stove in a frying pan (adding a lid for faster melting), I roast my marshmallow using the kit. This system works great and makes it easy to remove either component from the heat if necessary.

If you have a gas stove, you can also scrap the kit entirely and roast your marsh-mallow by the flame of one burner while you melt ingredients in a frying pan over a second burner. I use low heat for melting ingredients, and medium to medium-low for marshmallow-roasting—but every stove is different, so adjust your settings as needed.

microwave

If you want a s'more fast, the microwave is for you! It takes just 7–10 seconds to "roast" a marshmallow or melt ingredients in the microwave. The marshmallows will not really be roasted, of course, and they will lack the slightly crisp texture of their golden-brown cousins. But they will be puffy and soft, and just fine for a quick treat. (Don't heat marshmallows longer than 10 seconds or they will get immensely sticky and rubbery.)

other cooking tips

roasting marshmallows

Some people like their marshmallows raw, others burned, but the consensus seems to be that golden brown works best. Creating these treats takes patience. The perfect soft, unscalded marshmallow comes from steady rotation near a heat source, ideally a coal-bed. For the most even roast, use a metal cooking rod or coat hanger—and of course a steady hand. Regular ol' sticks are fine too, though they tend to be curved or kinky, which can make marshmallows cook unevenly. Metal devices will cook marshmallows faster than wooden ones and are more likely to deliver gooey centers.

timing

Ideally, you want your ingredients to be melted at exactly the same time your marshmallow finishes roasting. To accomplish this feat, you must assess your heat source and cooking setup and adjust your timing accordingly. It's a good idea to do a tester s'more or two so you can figure out how long roasting and melting will take before you begin heavy production.

GENERAL PRINCIPLES TO KEEP IN MIND:

◆ Coals cook faster and more consistently than flames.
◆ Marshmallows cook faster on a metal cooking rod or coat hanger than on a stick or wooden rod.
◆ The more ingredients you use at once, the longer they will take to melt.
◆ The farther away from the heat source your ingredients are, the longer they will take to melt. (Okay, I know this one is obvious, but it still has to be part of your mental calculation.)

Therefore, if you are roasting marshmallows over coals but melting ingredients over a built-in grate that's a foot above the fire, you'll need to start melting those ingredients several minutes before you begin roasting the marshmallow. Again, you'll have to assess your individual situation each time, but it's not hard to get a basic idea of what will work and try it out. And even if you don't achieve perfection, the results will be tasty no matter what.

division of labor

Especially in a campfire scenario, the whole procedure seems to work best when one person handles the marshmallow roasting and everyone else can worry about assembling and melting the contents of their own s'mores. Things can get a bit hairy when you're trying to hold a plate, a pan, a spatula, and a stick at the same time.

Fortunately for me, my brother Dustin is a world-class marshmallow roaster, and we all let him handle that portion of the proceedings entirely. His standards are so high that he will destroy a marshmallow if it isn't perfectly golden and melty, even at the cries and protests of hungry friends. I know some people like to do it all themselves, but I personally like to concentrate on my ingredients, knowing that one of Dustin's perfect marshmallows will soon be melting upon them.

making your own recipes

In this book I've offered you many recipes beloved by friends and family, but the boundaries of my imagination shouldn't limit your experience. I encourage you to invent your own recipes, but there is a bit of danger in this (especially in conjunction with a buffet), as many people go a bit haywire and try to fit every kind of chocolate and topping on one s'more. Usually this approach is more stimulating to the eyes than to the palate; overloading a s'more with too many flavors tends to cancel them out. In general, it's much better to keep it simple—try one kind of new chocolate with one or *maybe* two additions. People do get distressed at the thought that they won't be able to try everything, but it helps to keep faith that there will be another opportunity and another buffet in one's future.

sweet starts

fruit flavor burst

THIS S'MORE WAS THE VERY FIRST ONE I EVER MADE. IT'S ONE OF THE SIMPLEST, YET ONE OF THE BEST.

Milk chocolate

1 graham cracker, broken in half

1 marshmallow

1 slice strawberry, peach, or mango,
*   about 1/2 to 1 inch thick*

Arrange chocolate on half of the graham cracker and melt (see page 15). Roast the marshmallow. Once the chocolate has melted, remove graham cracker from heat and layer with fruit and roasted marshmallow. Top off with remaining graham cracker.

note: *The best way to make this s'more is to use one fruit slice of uniform thickness that will cover as much of the graham cracker as possible. If you don't mind a messier eating experience, you can use several thinner slices of fruit instead (which may slide out when you take a bite). However you slice it, choose the juiciest and most flavorful fruit for the best possible s'more!*

rocky road

JUST SWAP OUT THE PLAIN CHOCOLATE FOR AN INSTANT NUTTY
VARIATION ON THE ORIGINAL.

Milk chocolate with almonds

1 graham cracker, broken in half

1 marshmallow

No tricks here! Arrange chocolate on half of the graham cracker and melt (see page 15). Roast the marshmallow. Once the chocolate has melted, remove graham cracker from heat and top with roasted marshmallow and remaining graham cracker.

variation: *If you're out of nutty chocolate, just top plain milk chocolate with sliced unsalted almonds.*

milky way melt

WITH ITS FLUFFY NOUGAT AND CARAMEL, THIS CREAMY S'MORE MAY LAUNCH YOU RIGHT OUT OF THIS WORLD.

4 Milky Way Minis, regular or dark
1 graham cracker, broken in half
1 marshmallow

Distribute the Milky Way Minis evenly on half of the graham cracker and melt (see page 15). Because the chocolate is thinner than a regular chocolate bar, you won't need to heat your s'more as long as usual. Roast the marshmallow. When candy bar pieces are sufficiently gooey, remove graham cracker from heat, add roasted marshmallow and top with remaining graham cracker.

variations: *You can also, of course, make this s'more with a graham cracker-size piece of a standard Milky Way bar. I prefer the bite-size Minis because they are easier to spread evenly over the graham cracker, and I like mixing the light and dark varieties in the same s'more. But the essential flavor can be achieved either way.*

If you don't want quite so much nougat, you can use 2 Milky Way Minis and fill in the rest of the graham cracker with regular chocolate bar pieces.

simple mint

MINT LOVERS, START MELTING! THIS MINT MEDLEY FEATURES VELVETY ANDES MINTS AND A CRISPY MINT COOKIE.

3 to 4 Andes mints

1/2 graham cracker

1 marshmallow

1 crispy mint cookie (Thin Mint, Mint Oreo, Mint Brussels, etc.)

Unwrap mints and melt them on the graham cracker (see page 15). Roast the marshmallow. Once the chocolate has melted, remove graham cracker from heat and top with roasted marshmallow and mint cookie.

note: *The Andes mint is the nobility of the mint world. With its creamy consistency, high meltability, and luscious flavor, the Andes mint can be incorporated into almost any s'more for unbelievable results. For a stronger flavor of fresh peppermint, swap out the Andes mints for two squares of a delicious After Eight candy bar.*

sugar cookie crunch

CRISPY RICE IN A SUGARY CLOUD OF MARSHMALLOW AND WHITE CHOCOLATE.

Nestle Crunch White

2 sugar cookies

1 marshmallow

Arrange the chocolate on one sugar cookie and melt (see page 15). Keep heat low and watch carefully—sugar cookies can burn quickly! Roast the marshmallow. Once the chocolate has melted, remove cookie from heat and top with roasted marshmallow and remaining cookie.

simple orange

Have some delicious citrus with orange chocolate and an orange-filled biscuit.

Orange chocolate
1/2 graham cracker
1 marshmallow
1 Pim's orange biscuit

Arrange the chocolate on the graham cracker and begin melting (see page 15). Roast the marshmallow. Once the chocolate has melted, remove graham cracker from heat and top with roasted marshmallow and orange biscuit.

chewy apricot

Texture is everything in this s'more, which combines smooth melted dark chocolate with chewy dried fruit.

Dark chocolate
1 graham cracker, broken in half
1 marshmallow
2 or 3 dried apricots

Arrange chocolate on half of the graham cracker and melt (see page 15). Roast the marshmallow. Once chocolate has melted, remove graham cracker from heat and secure apricots in chocolate. Top with roasted marshmallow and remaining graham cracker.

the fluffernutter

THE FLUFFERNUTTER MAY BE A FAIRLY BIZARRE SANDWICH, BUT THE COMBINATION OF PEANUT BUTTER, CHOCOLATE AND MARSHMALLOW MAKES ONE HEAVENLY S'MORE!

1 Reese's peanut butter cup

1 graham cracker, broken in half

1 marshmallow

Place the peanut butter cup on half of the graham cracker and melt (see page 15). Roast the marshmallow. Once peanut butter cup has melted, remove graham cracker from heat and top with roasted marshmallow and remaining graham cracker.

variation: *Add four slices of banana. For stability's sake, your best bet is to place the banana slices on the graham cracker, then add the peanut butter cup on top of that—though this arrangement will take longer to melt the chocolate. You can also add the bananas on top of the peanut butter cup after melting, but take care not to lose the bananas as you take a bite!*

the chocoholic

A RICH SANDWICH OF CHOCOLATE COOKIES, MELTED CHOCOLATE, AND EVEN A CHOCOLATE MARSHMALLOW, THIS S'MORE IS A CHOCOHOLIC'S DREAM.

Milk or dark chocolate

2 large soft dark chocolate cookies

1 marshmallow, chocolate or regular

Arrange the chocolate on one cookie and melt (see page 15). If necessary, place second cookie over heat to soften. Roast the marshmallow. Once the chocolate has melted, remove cookie from heat and top with roasted marshmallow and remaining cookie.

banana caramel

MOLTEN CARAMEL, CREAMY CHOCOLATE AND SWEET BANANA COME
TOGETHER IN THIS GOOEY AND DELICIOUS S'MORE.

2 to 3 Hershey's Caramel Kisses

1 graham cracker, broken in half

1 marshmallow

4 banana slices

Arrange the Kisses on half of the graham cracker and melt (see page 15). The chocolate is properly melted when it begins to become soft and wet-looking—take care that you do not over-melt the chocolate, as the caramel filling can escape and spill. Roast the marshmallow. Once the chocolate has melted, remove graham cracker from heat and add sliced bananas, pressing them into the chocolate carefully. Add roasted marshmallow and top with remaining graham cracker.

variations: Omit the Kisses and use plain milk chocolate or milk chocolate with almonds. Top the chocolate and bananas with caramel syrup before adding the roasted marshmallow.

For a dramatic presentation, create a "banana boat" by using one large banana slice (as shown in the photo) instead of four small ones.

the antioxidant

Blueberries and dark chocolate contain antioxidants, which may help protect our cells against aging and disease. Feel good about snacking when you choose this delicious antioxidant-rich s'more! This recipe was contributed by Leigh Ann Maze.

Dark chocolate

1 graham cracker, broken in half

1 marshmallow

Fresh blueberries

Arrange the chocolate on half of the graham cracker and melt (see page 15). Roast the marshmallow. Once the chocolate has melted, remove graham cracker from heat and place fresh blueberries on chocolate, tapping to secure. Top with roasted marshmallow and remaining graham cracker.

german chocolate

THIS S'MORE IS THE PERFECT GOOEY INDULGENCE FOR COCONUT LOVERS, WITH OR WITHOUT CHOPPED PECANS.

Mounds candy bar, cut to fit on a
  graham cracker half
1 graham cracker, broken in half
1 marshmallow
Chopped pecans (optional)

Arrange the candy bar on half of the graham cracker and melt (see page 15). Roast the marshmallow. Once the candy bar has melted, remove graham cracker from heat and add chopped pecans, if using. Top with the marshmallow and remaining graham cracker.

variation: *If you like nuts but don't have pecans around, swap your Mounds for an Almond Joy.*

the two-tone

THIS RECIPE IS ALL ABOUT CONTRAST: EXPERIMENT WITH FLAVOR, TEXTURE, OR TEMPERATURE BY CHOOSING ONE DISTINCT TOPPING FOR EACH HALF OF YOUR S'MORE.

2 distinct fruits, chocolates or candy toppings of choice*

1 graham cracker, broken in half

1 marshmallow

*tasty topping combinations:

White and dark chocolate
Melted and unmelted chocolate
Melted chocolate and chilled fruit
Strawberries and bananas
Caramel and chocolate
Orange and white chocolate
Peaches and blackberries
Dried and fresh fruit
Lavender and white chocolate

Arrange the two toppings of choice on half of the graham cracker, and melt if desired (see page 15). Roast the marshmallow. Once both components are ready, top with the roasted marshmallow, taking care not to mix the two toppings. Finish off with the remaining graham cracker.

raspberry-fig bar

You don't even need chocolate in this tasty s'more that combines tangy raspberry and sweet fig.

2 dried figs, stems removed

4 fresh raspberries

1 graham cracker, broken in half

1 marshmallow

Cut each fig into small pieces and cut each raspberry in half. Arrange fig pieces evenly on graham cracker and then top with raspberry halves. Roast the marshmallow. Once the marshmallow is roasted, slide it onto the fruit and top with the remaining graham cracker.

cornflake crunch

THIS S'MORE FEATURES A CRISP TEXTURE THAT DELIGHTFULLY
CONTRASTS THE MELTED CHOCOLATE AND MARSHMALLOW.

Milk chocolate

1 graham cracker, broken in half

1 marshmallow

*Cornflakes (or a crispy cereal of
your choice)*

Arrange the chocolate on half of the graham cracker and melt (see page 15). Roast the marshmallow. Once the chocolate has melted, remove graham cracker from heat and sprinkle cornflakes over chocolate. Top with roasted marshmallow and remaining graham cracker.

variation: *You can also use chocolate already filled with cornflakes—the flakes will stay crisp even as the chocolate melts. See page 125 for a list of specialty chocolate brands.*

melon refresher

MELON AND CHOCOLATE IS AN UNUSUAL PAIRING, BUT NOTHING COULD BE MORE SWEET AND THIRST-QUENCHING THAN THIS EASY-TO-MAKE S'MORE. IT'S A DELICIOUS AND SATISFYING DESSERT THAT'S NOT QUITE AS STICKY-SWEET AS A CHOCOLATE/CANDY COMBINATION.

1 slice chilled cantaloupe, cut to fit on a
   graham cracker half
Milk chocolate
1 graham cracker, broken in half
1 marshmallow

At least an hour before s'moring begins, cut a slice of cantaloupe (thickness is up to you, but try to use one piece rather than several slices) and wedge it next to something icy in the cooler (or, if you're at home, just pop it in the fridge). When it's time to make the s'more, arrange the chocolate on half of the graham cracker and melt (see page 15). Roast the marshmallow. Once the chocolate has melted, remove graham cracker from heat. Place the chilled melon over the chocolate and top with the roasted marshmallow and remaining graham cracker.

classic tastes

cookie dough

THIS S'MORE IS EVEN MORE TEMPTING AND SATISFYING THAN LICKING
THE COOKIE-BATTER BOWL.

1 marshmallow

2 soft chocolate chip cookies

Chocolate chip cookie dough
  (homemade or store-bought)

Roast the marshmallow and warm the cookies to soften, if desired. Spread a layer of cookie dough on one cookie (1/2 inch should be perfect for most, but hardcore cookie dough lovers may prefer to use more). Top with marshmallow and remaining cookie.

note: *Though cookie dough has a distinct flavor, for some reason it tends to get lost in s'mores, especially if combined with several other flavors. This s'more, however, manages to isolate both the taste of the baked cookie and the dough. If you love cookie dough, this is a must-try!*

strawberry shortcake

NOTHING SAYS SUMMER LIKE THIS LIGHT AND CREAMY DESSERT.

2 yellow strawberry shortcake cups

Fresh sliced strawberries

1 marshmallow

Fill one shortcake cup with strawberry slices. Roast the marshmallow. Once marshmallow is done, slide it into remaining shortcake cup. Carefully invert the cup with marshmallow and place it atop the cup with strawberries.

bananas foster

CONJURE UP THIS FAMOUS FLAMING DESSERT AT YOUR CAMPFIRE OR IN THE KITCHEN.

4 banana slices

Cinnamon

Milk or dark chocolate

1 graham cracker, broken in half

1 marshmallow

Splash of rum (optional)

Sprinkle banana slices with cinnamon on both sides. Arrange the chocolate on half of the graham cracker and melt (see page 15). Roast the marshmallow. Once the chocolate has melted, remove graham cracker from heat and add the bananas and roasted marshmallow. Quickly dip one flat side of the remaining graham cracker half in rum, if using. Top the s'more with rummy graham cracker.

note: *If you're the sort who loves burned marshmallows, try it with this one. Real Bananas Foster always has flames!*

mexican chocolate

THIS CINNAMON-CHOCOLATE S'MORE IS A WARM AND SUGARY DELIGHT. CALL IT BY ITS SPANISH NAME: S'MAS!

1 marshmallow

Cinnamon

Milk chocolate

1/2 graham cracker

1 soft snickerdoodle

Roll the marshmallow in cinnamon, coating evenly. Arrange the chocolate on the graham cracker and melt (see page 15). Roast the marshmallow. Caution: cinnamon-rolled marshmallows may catch fire more easily than non-coated ones, so pay special attention while roasting, and keep the marshmallow a little farther from the heat than you normally would. When the marshmallow is almost done, heat the cookie to soften. Once the chocolate has melted, remove graham cracker from heat and top with roasted marshmallow and cookie.

variation: For even more cinnamon flavor, use half of a cinnamon Pop-Tart instead of a snickerdoodle. But be careful—Pop-Tarts fall apart when warm.

best brownies

Brownies are scrumptious in s'mores, and you can vary almost any recipe in this book by substituting a brownie for a top graham cracker. If you love brownies, be creative!

When working with brownies, keep in mind a few things. Brownies tend to be thick with a rich flavor. If you sandwich two brownies together, you won't always be able to taste whatever you have enclosed within them. Instead, use a graham cracker on the bottom and a brownie on the top. The graham cracker also enables you to melt toppings more easily. If cooking with a lidded pan, you should be able to melt toppings on a brownie bottom, but if you're cooking directly on a campfire or grill, your brownie might crumble into the fire or never get hot enough to melt any toppings. Finally, brownies have such a strong flavor that you don't always need a whole one to top your s'more; cut a smaller square and you'll still be delighted without overwhelming the other flavors you've chosen.

Oh, one more note: plain brownies work well, but these treats also come in many varieties and you should feel free to use your favorite.

hazelnut raspberry brownie

THIS CLASSY S'MORE PAIRS LUSCIOUS NUTELLA TOPPING WITH FRESH RASPBERRIES AND TOPS IT ALL WITH A DELICIOUS BROWNIE SQUARE.

1/2 graham cracker

Nutella

4 fresh raspberries

1 marshmallow

1 brownie square

Slather the graham cracker generously with Nutella and then add raspberries, tapping to secure. Roast the marshmallow. Top graham cracker with roasted marshmallow and brownie square.

minty brownie

FOR AN INCREDIBLE CHOCOLATE-MINT S'MORE, FOLD COOL, CREAMY MINTS AND FLUFFY MARSHMALLOW INSIDE A RICH BROWNIE SANDWICH.

1 marshmallow

A handful of Junior Mints

2 brownie squares OR 1 brownie
  square and 1/2 graham cracker

Roast the marshmallow. If desired, melt mints on the brownie bottom or graham cracker half (see page 15). Once the mints have melted, remove brownie or graham cracker from heat. Add roasted marshmallow and top with remaining brownie square.

note: *While all meltable mints are a s'more-lover's friend, Junior Mints work wonderfully with brownies because they are gooey without melting, and their flavor is strong enough to complement even the most chocolatey brownie.*

butterscotch-butterfinger brownie

CROWNED WITH A CHOCOLATE BROWNIE, THIS S'MORE FEATURES A
CREAMY-CRISPY CENTER OF MELTED BUTTERSCOTCH CHIPS AND
CHOPPED BUTTERFINGER PIECES.

Butterscotch chips

1/2 graham cracker

1 marshmallow

*Small piece of Butterfinger bar, loosely
chopped*

1 brownie square

Arrange the butterscotch chips on the graham
cracker and melt (see page 15). Roast the
marshmallow. Once the butterscotch chips
have melted, remove graham cracker from
heat and sprinkle Butterfinger pieces over
melted butterscotch. Top with roasted marshmallow and brownie square.

cookies & cream brownie

SMOOTH, CRUNCHY, AND CHEWY ALL AT ONCE, THIS YUMMY TREAT COMBINES WHITE CHOCOLATE, CHOCOLATE COOKIE PIECES, AND ROASTED MARSHMALLOW, ALL BENEATH A BROWNIE SQUARE.

Hershey's Cookies 'n' Creme chocolate

1/2 graham cracker

1 marshmallow

1 brownie square

Arrange the chocolate on the graham cracker and melt (see page 15). Roast the marshmallow. Once the chocolate has melted, remove graham cracker from heat and top with roasted marshmallow and brownie.

lemon bar

THIS TALL S'MORE TASTES JUST LIKE THE LIGHT LEMONY BAKERY TREAT OF THE SAME NAME.

1 marshmallow

1 mini powdered donut

2 Pim's lemon mousse biscuits

Roast the marshmallow. When done, place the donut on one biscuit. Top the donut with the roasted marshmallow and then finish with remaining biscuit.

john's jelly donut

A DELICIOUSLY LIGHT S'MORE WITH RASPBERRY FILLING AND POWDERED SUGAR.

1 marshmallow

1 mini powdered donut

2 Pim's raspberry biscuits

Roast the marshmallow. Place the donut on one biscuit. Top the donut with the roasted marshmallow and remaining biscuit.

variation: *For extra fruit flavor, place one or two fresh raspberries on the donut before adding the marshmallow.*

boston cream pie

LET THE MARSHMALLOW DO THE WORK OF THE CUSTARD IN THIS
FORKLESS VERSION OF THE YELLOW CAKE CLASSIC.

Chocolate frosting

2 yellow strawberry shortcake cups

1 marshmallow

Fill one shortcake cup with a scoop of chocolate frosting. Roast the marshmallow. When marshmallow is roasted, slide it into the second shortcake cup. Sandwich the two shortcake cups together and enjoy!

kettle corn

LOVE SALTY-SWEET SNACKS? JUST PAIR HERSHEY'S CARAMEL KISSES WITH FRESHLY POPPED BUTTERED POPCORN TO GET THAT KETTLE CORN TASTE.

3 Hershey's Caramel Kisses
1 graham cracker, broken in half
1 marshmallow
Fresh salted and buttered popcorn

Arrange the Kisses on half of the graham cracker, and melt (see page 15). Roast the marshmallow. Once Kisses look melted or wet, remove graham cracker from heat and press pieces of popcorn into the melted chocolate and caramel. Top with roasted marshmallow and remaining graham cracker.

s'blime

THIS S'MORE FEATURES THREE WAYS TO LIVEN UP YOUR DESSERT WITH TANGY LIME.

Lime-flavored chocolate
1 graham cracker, broken in half
1 marshmallow
Juice of 1 lime
Zest of 1 lime

Arrange the chocolate on half of the graham cracker and melt (see page 15). Roll the marshmallow in lime juice (briefly—it will dissolve if left too long) and roast. Once the chocolate has melted, remove graham cracker from heat and sprinkle lime zest over chocolate. Add roasted marshmallow and top with remaining graham cracker.

variations: *You can use less lime and still have a tasty s'more. Lime-flavored chocolate alone is delicious, as is zest or juice with plain chocolate. Or try using lemons! While I have never found a workable lemon-flavored chocolate, you could easily use plain chocolate while following the same procedure with lemon zest and juice. You could also use a lemon-filled chocolate candy (made by See's, Godiva, and others).*

ilima's favorite fruit smoothie

VARIETY IS THE SPICE OF THIS FRUITFUL S'MORE. STACK UP YOUR FAVORITE FLAVORS FOR A TALL TREAT THAT TASTES SCRUMPTIOUS WITH OR WITHOUT CHOCOLATE.

Orange chocolate (optional)

1/2 graham cracker

1 marshmallow

Fruit slices and berries of your choice
  (strawberries, bananas, raspberries,
  mango, etc.)

1 Pim's orange or raspberry biscuit

If you're adding chocolate . . .
Arrange the chocolate on the graham cracker and melt (see page 15). Roast the marshmallow. When chocolate is soft, remove graham cracker from heat and add the fruit, tapping to secure in the melted chocolate. Add roasted marshmallow and top with the biscuit.

If you're not adding chocolate . . .
Stack up your fruit selections on the graham cracker with the most stable on the bottom. Roast the marshmallow. When the marshmallow is ready, add it to the fruit stack and top with the biscuit.

tracey's caramel apple

THIS TART, CHEWY, JUICY S'MORE IS EVEN BETTER THAN THE CARNIVAL FAVORITE.

1 marshmallow

2 chewy caramels

2 green apple slices, about 1/2 inch thick

Skewer the marshmallow followed by the two caramels on the same roasting stick. Roast the marshmallow and caramels. When the caramels have melted over the top of the marshmallow, and the marshmallow is cooked to your liking, slide the concoction onto one of the apple slices. Top with remaining apple slice.

variation: *For a cute presentation, use apple tops with stems (as shown in the photo) to complete these s'mores.*

piña colada

A CLASSIC DRINK BECOMES AN UNFORGETTABLE S'MORE. NO UMBRELLA REQUIRED!

1 soft macaroon

Splash of rum (optional)

Milk or dark chocolate

1/2 graham cracker

1 slice pineapple, about 1/2 inch thick

1 marshmallow

Briefly dip the flat side of the macaroon in the rum, if using. Arrange the chocolate on the graham cracker, top with pineapple, and melt (see page 15). Roast the marshmallow. Once the chocolate has melted, remove graham cracker from heat. Top with roasted marshmallow and macaroon.

variation: *No macaroons? Use a Mounds candy bar instead of plain chocolate.*

coffee talk

There are many varieties of coffee-flavored chocolate—almost every specialty chocolatier makes one—and some are stronger than others. When combining coffee-flavored chocolate with other flavored chocolates (as in the Biscotti Latte recipe below), be sure to taste them all before you begin so you can determine the right proportions for each. Ideally, you'll want to achieve a balance of the two flavors, which may require you to use more of one chocolate and less of another.

biscotti latte

CREATE YOUR FAVORITE LATTE BY BLENDING COFFEE-FLAVORED CHOCOLATE WITH VANILLA, CARAMEL, OR MINT.

1 biscotto

1/2 graham cracker

Coffee-flavored chocolate

Vanilla white chocolate, Andes mint, or Hershey's Caramel Kiss

1 marshmallow

variation: *For a dramatic, extra-large treat, use a full graham cracker and unbroken biscotto (as shown in the photo).*

Break off a piece of biscotto about as long as the graham cracker and set aside. Break chocolate selections into small pieces and arrange on graham cracker (if you're using a Kiss, place in the middle of graham cracker and arrange coffee chocolate around it). Melt the chocolate (see page 15) and roast the marshmallow. Once the chocolate has melted, remove graham cracker from heat. If desired, stir chocolate slightly with a toothpick or knife to mix. Top with roasted marshmallow and biscotto.

coffee plus

THIS GROWN-UP S'MORE FEATURES COFFEE-FLAVORED CHOCOLATE, FLUFFY MARSHMALLOW, AND YOUR FAVORITE ALCOHOLIC ADDITIVE.

*Kahlua, Irish Cream, brandy, or other
  favorite alcoholic additive*
Coffee-flavored chocolate
1 graham cracker, broken in half
1 marshmallow

Pour a bit of the alcoholic additive into a saucer or small bowl and set aside. Arrange the chocolate on half of the graham cracker and melt (see page 15). Roast the marshmallow. Once the chocolate has melted, remove graham cracker from heat and slide marshmallow onto chocolate. Dip one flat side of the remaining graham cracker into the alcoholic additive to coat. Place graham cracker on top of roasted marshmallow, alcohol-side down. Eat responsibly!

coffee toffee

With its melted coffee-flavored chocolate and toffee-bar top, this s'more satisfies both coffee and candy cravings.

Coffee-flavored chocolate

1/2 graham cracker

1 marshmallow

1 piece toffee candy bar (such as a Heath or Skor bar), cut the same length as the graham cracker

Arrange the chocolate on the graham cracker and melt (see page 15). Roast the marshmallow. Once the chocolate has melted, remove graham cracker from heat and slide the roasted marshmallow onto chocolate. Top with the toffee bar.

intense espresso

NEED A SUGAR FIX AND A CAFFEINE BOOST? EACH BITE OF THIS S'MORE DELIVERS A POWERFUL BURST OF INTENSE ESPRESSO FLAVOR.

1 graham cracker, broken in half

Nutella or chocolate of your choice

1 marshmallow

6 chocolate-covered espresso beans

Cover half of the graham cracker with a thin layer of Nutella, or melt a small amount of chocolate on the cracker and spread it evenly over the surface. Roast the marshmallow. Tap the espresso beans in the Nutella or melted chocolate to secure. Add roasted marshmallow and top with remaining graham cracker.

note: *The chocolate layer in this s'more is there simply to cement the espresso beans, so Nutella is the easiest option, but you can also melt a thin layer of chocolate on the graham cracker half. Just don't use too much—you don't want to overpower the espresso flavor.*

extreme variations

s'more inside a s'more

THIS ONE IS TASTY, BUT IT MAY ALSO BLOW YOUR MIND. IT'S A S'MORE INSIDE A S'MORE INSIDE A S'MORE . . .

Milk chocolate

1 frosted S'more Pop Tart, cut in half

1 Hershey's S'mores bar, cut in thirds

1 marshmallow

Arrange the milk chocolate on the frosted side of half of the Pop Tart, then place 2 pieces of the S'mores bar on top of the chocolate. Eat the remaining piece of the S'mores bar or give it to someone deserving. Melt the chocolate if you like (see page 15), but not too long because Pop Tarts are fragile (for more resilience, use a regular graham cracker for the bottom piece). Roast the marshmallow. Once the chocolate has melted, remove Pop Tart or graham cracker from heat. Top with roasted marshmallow and remaining Pop Tart.

the peanut butter slob

THIS S'MORE PERFECTLY ILLUSTRATES THE SIMPLICITY PRINCIPLE: JUST TWO INGREDIENTS, BUT OH SO GOOD. DON'T FORGET THE NAPKINS!

2 Reese's peanut butter cups

1 marshmallow

Unwrap the peanut butter cups and set aside. Roast the marshmallow. Once the marshmallow is roasted, sandwich it between the peanut butter cups. Eat quickly before it melts all over!

variation: *For a slightly less slobby version, use one Reese's Big Cup instead of two regular ones, sliding your marshmallow on top. Eat this variation like an open-faced sandwich. If you want, you can even scoop out some of the peanut butter filling and add another kind of candy, such as M&Ms or chopped Butterfinger pieces.*

emma's pound cake spectacular

A SANDWICH OF POUND CAKE, NUTELLA, STRAWBERRIES, AND MARSH-
MALLOW—FIT FOR THE GODS!

2 slices pound cake, about 1/2 inch thick

Nutella

Sliced strawberries

1 marshmallow

Generously cover one side of each pound cake slice with Nutella. Arrange strawberries over Nutella on one slice. Roast the marshmallow. Once the marshmallow is roasted, place it atop the strawberries. Top with second pound cake slice, Nutella-side down.

variation: *For even more goodness, try toasting and buttering the pound cake before spreading it with Nutella.*

stuffed apricot

A JUICY APRICOT MAKES A PERFECT S'MORE CONTAINER THAT'S FLAVORFUL, EASY TO EAT, AND EVEN A BIT HEALTHIER THAN YOUR AVERAGE S'MORE.

1 apricot

Chocolate syrup

1 marshmallow

Chocolate chips or chocolate slivers

Slice the apricot in half along its natural seam and remove the pit. Swirl a bit of chocolate syrup on each half of the apricot. Make a few incisions in the marshmallow and insert the chocolate pieces (see page 17). Roast the marshmallow, taking care not to lose the melting chocolate. Once the marshmallow is roasted and chocolate is melted, sandwich the marshmallow between the two apricot halves.

chocolate raspberry croissant

CHOCOLATE CROISSANTS ARE GOOD. S'MORE CROISSANTS ARE WAY BETTER.

1 plain croissant

Dark chocolate

1 marshmallow

Fresh raspberries

Cut croissant in half lengthwise, making the bottom half thinner than the top half. Arrange the chocolate on the bottom half of the croissant and melt (see page 15). Happily, the butter in the pastry will keep it from burning. Roast the marshmallow. Once the chocolate has melted, remove croissant from heat and tap raspberries into the chocolate to secure. Top with roasted marshmallow and the top half of the croissant.

the waffler

WAFFLES AND MAPLE SYRUP ARE NOT JUST FOR BREAKFAST ANYMORE! THIS CRISPY-SWEET S'MORE WILL CURE A MAPLE CRAVING ANY TIME OF DAY.

1 toaster waffle or homemade waffle,
   cut in half
1 marshmallow
Maple syrup

Heat the waffle halves on the grill or in the toaster—the crispier, the better! Roast the marshmallow. Once the marshmallow is ready, slide it onto one of the waffle halves. Drizzle maple syrup over roasted marshmallow to taste. Top with remaining waffle half and enjoy!

variation: *Add your favorite fruit topping, such as cinnamon apples, berries, or bananas, to the bottom waffle before adding the marshmallow and maple syrup.*

note: *Don't try to coat your marshmallow with syrup before roasting. The syrup acts as a shield while the marshmallow remains uncooked—and eventually the syrup just heats up and drips off. Better to add the syrup after the cooking!*

black forest cupcake

A CHOCOLATE CUPCAKE FILLED WITH FRESH CHERRIES, CREAMY CHOCOLATE, AND SMOOTH MARSHMALLOW.

1 chocolate cupcake, unfrosted

1 to 2 fresh cherries, pitted and sliced

5 to 10 chocolate chips

1 marshmallow

Scoop out a hole in your cupcake large enough to hold a roasted marshmallow (it's easiest just to pick out the cake and eat it). Place the cherry slices in the bottom of the cake cup and top with a few of the chocolate chips.

Make some incisions in the marshmallow and insert the remaining chocolate chips (see page 17). Roast the marshmallow, taking care not to lose the melting chocolate. Once the marshmallow is roasted and the chocolate is melted, add the marshmallow to the cake cup.

variations: *Omit the chocolate chips and top the sliced cherries with hot fudge. Or, for an elegant presentation, top each cupcake with a whole cherry, complete with stem (as shown).*

s'more parfait

THIS COMPLETELY EDIBLE PARFAIT CONTAINS THREE LAYERS OF CHOCO-
LATE, CANDY, OR FRUIT, AND TWO MARSHMALLOWS. YOU CAN USE A
DIFFERENT KIND OF CHOCOLATE, CANDY, OR FRUIT FOR EACH LAYER,
OR THE SAME ONE FOR ALL THREE.

Chocolate syrup (or syrup of any flavor)

1 ice cream cone (plain or sugar)

Candy or fruit of choice, chopped*

2 marshmallows

*try these yummy flavor combinations:

Oreo cookie pieces, chopped nuts, and sprinkles

Mixed berries and chocolate (all layers)

*Dark chocolate, espresso beans, chopped
    biscotti pieces*

Chopped peaches, blueberries, strawberries

Strawberries, Mounds bar, pineapple

*Chocolate with rice crisps, chocolate with nuts,
    chocolate with cornflakes*

Dark chocolate, milk chocolate, white chocolate

Andes mint, Junior Mint, Peppermint Pattie

Drizzle the syrup on the inside of ice cream cone to coat. Put a small amount of candy or fruit in the bottom of the cone. Roast the marshmallows. Once the marshmallows are roasted, insert one into the cone, using a knife or spoon to push the marshmallow as far into the cone as possible. Top with a second layer of candy or fruit. Add second roasted marshmallow and top with final layer of candy or fruit.

note: *You can also convert almost every recipe in this book to parfait form simply by chopping and layering the ingredients in an ice cream cone.*

variation: *For a giant-size parfait, use a waffle cone and create as many marshmallow/candy layers as you can. Flavored marshmallows work great!*

reverse s'more

1 Hostess Ding-Dong

1 marshmallow

1/2 graham cracker

Carefully cut the Ding-Dong lengthwise and separate into two round pieces (you may lose some frosting or aesthetic value, but don't worry—it'll still taste good). Roast the marshmallow. Once the marshmallow is roasted, place the graham cracker on bottom half of the Ding-Dong. Add roasted marshmallow and top with remaining Ding-Dong half.

banana nut muffin

THIS DELICIOUS, HEARTY TREAT IS S'MORE FILLING THAN OTHER VARIETIES.

Milk chocolate or chocolate with nuts
of your choice

1/2 graham cracker

1 marshmallow

4 banana slices

1 banana nut muffin top

Arrange the chocolate on half of the graham cracker and melt (see page 15). Roast the marshmallow. Once the chocolate has melted, remove graham cracker from heat and add the banana slices to the chocolate. Top with roasted marshmallow and muffin top.

note: *A regular-size muffin works best for this s'more. Larger muffin tops can overpower the other flavors.*

variations: *Use any muffin type you like and pair it with complementary toppings. Add blueberries and chocolate to a blueberry muffin, apples and caramel to an apple muffin, etc. If you don't want to melt the chocolate, you can also exchange the graham cracker for a muffin bottom, or sandwich two muffin tops together.*

katy's krispy treat

IF YOU THOUGHT S'MORES COULDN'T GET ANY SWEETER, THINK AGAIN.
TRY THIS IF YOU REALLY WANT A MARSHMALLOW FIX.

1 Rice Krispies Treat

Nutella

Strawberries, raspberries or peaches,
   sliced (optional)

1 marshmallow

Slice the Rice Krispies Treat in half length-wise. Spread one half with Nutella and top with fruit, if using. Roast the marshmallow. Once the marshmallow is roasted, add it to the bottom slice and then top with remaining Rice Krispies Treat slice.

variations: *If you don't have any Nutella handy or want to use regular chocolate, try inserting chocolate chips into your marshmallow before you roast (see page 17). Do not attempt to melt the chocolate on the Rice Krispies Treat—it will quickly melt or burn! Or, for even more chocolate, go with a Cocoa Krispies Treat instead of the original.*

hardcore mint

FOR DEDICATED MINT FANS ONLY. EAT THIS S'MORE FAST FOR THE BIGGEST MINT RUSH.

2 giant-size Peppermint Patties

1 marshmallow

Unwrap the peppermint patties and set aside. Roast the marshmallow. Once the marshmallow is roasted, sandwich it between the peppermint patties. Eat quickly before it melts all over!

the exotics

toasted coconut caramel

TOASTED COCONUT, CARAMEL AND CHOCOLATE—CROWNED WITH A DELICIOUS SAMOA GIRL SCOUT COOKIE.

2 to 3 Hershey's Caramel Kisses

1/2 graham cracker

1 Jet-Puffed Toasted Coconut marsh-
mallow (hard to find but worth it)

1 Samoa Girl Scout cookie

Arrange the Kisses on the graham cracker and melt (see page 15). Watch the Kisses carefully so that they just begin to melt; if overdone, the caramel can ooze out of the chocolate covering and spill or burn. Roast the marshmallow. Once the chocolate has melted, remove graham cracker from heat and top with roasted marshmallow. Finish with Samoa cookie. This s'more will work with a regular marshmallow, but the toasted coconut variety is truly delicious!

note: *Samoas (in the purple box) are sometimes packaged as Caramel De Lites (in the orange box), but they're the same cookie.*

marzi-pear

IF S'MORES WERE SERVED AT AFTERNOON TEA, THIS WOULD BE THE
RECIPE YOU'D FIND NESTLED AMONG THE CRUSTLESS SANDWICHES AND
PETITS FOURS.

2 to 4 cubes marzipan-filled chocolate
1 graham cracker, broken in half
1 marshmallow
1 slice fresh, ripe pear, about 1/2 inch thick

Arrange the marzipan chocolate on half of the graham cracker and melt (see page 15). Roast the marshmallow. Once chocolate has melted, remove graham cracker from heat and add the pear slice. Top with roasted marsh-mallow and remaining graham cracker.

variation: *For a creamier version, replace the pear slice with two Hershey's Caramel Kisses.*

the mint raspberry sophisticate

RASPBERRIES, CHOCOLATE, AND JUST A HINT OF MINT MELT TOGETHER IN THIS SIMPLE AND ELEGANT S'MORE.

3 to 4 Andes mints

1 graham cracker, broken in half

1 marshmallow

4 fresh raspberries

Arrange the mints evenly on half of the graham cracker and melt (see page 15). Roast the marshmallow. Once mints have melted, remove graham cracker from heat and add raspberries, lightly tapping to secure. Add roasted marshmallow and top with remaining graham cracker.

passion banana cream

THIS SMOOTH S'MORE FEATURES CREAMY VANILLA AND BANANA WITH A TROPICAL TWIST OF PASSION FRUIT.

Vanilla white chocolate

1 graham cracker, broken in half

1 marshmallow

4 banana slices

Passion fruit*

*Passion fruit has a strong and distinct flavor, so it adds a nice kick to this otherwise mellow s'more. How much passion fruit you use should depend on what role you want it to play in this recipe—I use it as a light sauce, but passion fruit fanatics may prefer to add it in more liberal quantities. I don't care for the seeds, so I try to use only the juice for this recipe; but the seeds will add an interesting crunch to the s'more, so keep them in if you like their taste.

Arrange the chocolate on half of the graham cracker and melt (see page 15). Roast the marshmallow. Once the chocolate has melted, remove graham cracker from heat and lightly press the banana slices in the chocolate. Drizzle passion fruit over the bananas. Add roasted marshmallow and top with remaining graham cracker.

maria's lavender lift

FLOWERS IN FOOD? WELL, SURE! IF IT'S DELICATE ELEGANCE YOU'RE AFTER, TRY THIS LIGHT AND AROMATIC S'MORE.

Lavender chocolate

2 lavender cookies OR 1 graham cracker, broken in half

1 marshmallow

Arrange the chocolate on a cookie or half of the graham cracker and melt (see page 15). Roast the marshmallow. Once the chocolate has melted, remove cookie or graham cracker from heat. Finish with roasted marshmallow and remaining cookie or graham cracker.

note: *If you're lucky like me, you have a friend who grows her own lavender and bakes it into crispy cookies. If you're not so lucky, you can find lavender cookies at select farmers' markets or specialty food stores, or bake your own by adding 1 tablespoon of ground culinary lavender to the creamed components (butter and sugar) of any basic sugar or butter cookie recipe. You can purchase culinary lavender at www.littleskylavender.com or from other lavender growers, many of whom sell their fragrant wares online. If that's too much of a hassle, just try lavender chocolate with good ol' graham crackers.*

variation: *If you're using lavender cookies, you can substitute milk, white, or marzipan chocolate for the lavender chocolate.*

stroopwafel taco

A Stroopwafel is a round Dutch wafer cookie with gooey maple or honey filling inside. Ingeniously designed to rest atop a mug, the Stroopwafel softens as the steam rises from the hot beverage within. But we don't need a mug or a hot beverage to turn this sweet cookie into an incredible s'more.

Hazelnut chocolate (preferably with
  hazelnut pieces)
1 Stroopwafel, any flavor
1 marshmallow

Arrange the chocolate on half of the Stroopwafel and melt (see page 15). Roast the marshmallow. Once the chocolate has melted and the Stroopwafel is soft, remove Stroopwafel from heat and slide the roasted marshmallow onto the melted chocolate. Fold the Stroopwafel in half and eat like a taco.

variation: This recipe is especially good with a crunchy chocolate—so if you don't like nuts, choose a chocolate containing rice crisps or cornflakes instead.

note: Hot Stroopwafels get droopy and difficult to handle, so it's best to heat them in a pan, not directly on a grill.

almond ginger melt

THE UNIQUE TASTE OF CANDIED GINGER, FOLDED BETWEEN CHOCO-
LATE AND ALMOND BUTTER LAYERS, SETS THIS S'MORE APART. THIS
RECIPE WAS CONTRIBUTED BY BONNIE AND NEVA STEWARD.

1 graham cracker, broken in half

Almond butter

Dark chocolate

1 marshmallow

1 s'more-size piece of dried candied ginger

Spread half of the graham cracker with almond butter and set aside. Arrange the chocolate on remaining graham cracker and melt (see page 15). Roast the marshmallow. Once the chocolate has melted, remove graham cracker from heat. Add ginger and roasted marshmallow. Top with the almond-buttered graham cracker.

note: *You can find candied ginger in most natural food stores, sometimes pre-packaged, sometimes in the bulk bins. You can also purchase chocolate-covered ginger—equally good in this recipe—from many chocolatiers.*

cinnamon chai

PERFECT FOR CHILLY WEATHER, THIS HEAVENLY S'MORE WARMS YOU UP ON THE INSIDE—JUST LIKE A CHAI LATTE.

Chai-flavored chocolate

1 graham cracker, broken in half

1 marshmallow

Cinnamon

Arrange the chocolate on half of the graham cracker and melt (see page 15). Roll the marshmallow in cinnamon to coat. Roast carefully, keeping the marshmallow a little farther from the fire than normal (cinnamon will make it easier to ignite the marshmallow, and the coating can also obscure a marshmallow's overly bronzed skin). Once the chocolate has melted, remove graham cracker from heat and top with roasted marshmallow and remaining graham cracker.

chocolate yogurt

THIS S'MORE BLENDS TANGY PLAIN YOGURT WITH THE SWEETNESS OF FRUIT OR HONEY AND THE CRUNCH OF GRANOLA.

Yogurt-filled chocolate

1 graham cracker, broken in half

1 marshmallow

Honey and/or sliced fruit (strawberries, raspberries, peaches, etc.)

Granola

Arrange the chocolate on half of the graham cracker and melt (see page 15). Melt only briefly, as the yogurt filling liquefies if completely melted and will attempt to run down your chin and spill everywhere. Roast the marshmallow. Once the chocolate has melted, remove graham cracker from heat and add roasted marshmallow. Drizzle with honey and/or add sliced fruit. Top with granola and remaining graham cracker.

orange pistachio

THIS NUTTY CITRUS COMBINATION IS SWEET, TART AND CRUNCHY ALL AT ONCE.

Orange chocolate

Pistachio-filled chocolate

1 graham cracker, broken in half

1 marshmallow

Slice or break up the two chocolate varieties into smaller pieces. Arrange chocolate evenly, mixing the two varieties, on half of the graham cracker and melt (see page 15). Roast the marshmallow. Once the chocolate has melted, remove graham cracker from heat and top with roasted marshmallow and remaining graham cracker.

holiday favorites

sweetheart s'more

WE ALL LOVE A BOX OF CHOCOLATES ON VALENTINE'S DAY, BUT IT'S EVEN BETTER TO SHARE A S'MORE WITH YOUR SWEETIE.

1 filled gourmet chocolate of choice
  (preferably soft-centered)
1 graham cracker, broken in half
1 marshmallow

Arrange the chocolate on half of the graham cracker and melt (see page 15). Roast the marshmallow. Once the chocolate begins to melt or glisten, remove graham cracker from heat and top with roasted marshmallow and remaining graham cracker.

shamrock s'more

EVERYTHING'S GREEN ON ST. PATRICK'S DAY, INCLUDING THIS AMAZING CHOCOLATE-MINT S'MORE.

Andes Mint Parfaits OR green mint chips
2 chocolate cookies with green mint chips
1 marshmallow

Arrange the mints on one cookie and melt (see page 15). Roast the marshmallow. Warm second cookie to soften, if desired. Once the mints have melted, remove cookie from heat and top with roasted marshmallow and second cookie.

the squashed chickie

CLASSIC MARSHMALLOW PEEPS ARE GOOD IN AN EASTER BASKET—BUT EVEN BETTER ON A STICK.

Milk chocolate (something from your
  Easter basket, if you like)
1 graham cracker, broken in half
1 Marshmallow Peep of any color

Arrange the chocolate on half of the graham cracker and melt (see page 15). Impale your Peep on a stick and heat very gently—keep it farther away from the heat than you would a regular marshmallow. The sugar will instantly begin to moisten and caramelize while the marshmallow filling liquifies. Remove Peep from heat and wait a few seconds; the cooling process will deliver a crispy outside shell for a nice creme brulee effect. Once the chocolate has melted, remove graham cracker from heat and top with roasted Peep and remaining graham cracker.

note: *Though we typically see the most of these Marshmallow Peeps around Easter, the Peeps folks also produce the same basic treats for other seasons and holidays. So you can also squash hearts, snowmen, ghosts and other cuddly characters all year round!*

the patriot

AT YOUR NEXT 4TH OF JULY BARBECUE, SCRAPE OFF THE GRILL AFTER DINNER AND MAKE SOME SPIRITED S'MORES FOR DESSERT.

Milk chocolate

1 graham cracker, broken in half

Fresh blueberries

1 marshmallow

1 thick strawberry slice, or 2 to 3
   smaller slices

Arrange the chocolate on half of the graham cracker. Set blueberries atop chocolate and melt (see page 15), being careful not to lose the blueberries in transport. Roast the marshmallow. Once chocolate has melted, remove graham cracker from heat and lightly tap blueberries to secure. Top with the strawberry slice(s), roasted marshmallow, and remaining graham cracker.

variation: *For the most spirited presentation, stack your ingredients in red, white, and blue order (as shown in the photo). Just be careful not to lose the strawberries when you take a bite!*

smashing pumpkins

THIS NOVEMBER, BE THANKFUL THAT YOU HAVE S'MORES IN YOUR
LIFE—AND TURN YOUR LEFTOVER PIE INTO THIS SEASONAL DELIGHT.

Vanilla or regular white chocolate

1 graham cracker, broken in half

1 marshmallow

Piece of pumpkin pie, cut to fit on
  graham cracker half*

Arrange the chocolate on half of the graham cracker and melt (see page 15). Roast the marshmallow. Once the chocolate has melted, remove graham cracker from heat and add pumpkin pie piece. Top with roasted marshmallow and remaining graham cracker.

*You can size your piece of pumpkin pie to suit your taste. For most, a slice 1 inch high should be perfect. Because pie is typically taller than that, I use a slice that's 1 inch wide and place it sideways on the graham cracker, However, for a more intense pumpkin flavor, you can use a taller piece of pie (as shown in the photo).

the saucy cranberry

CRANBERRY SAUCE IS USUALLY TOO TART FOR ME, BUT IT TASTES
DELICIOUS IN THIS S'MORE. THE MELTED VANILLA CHOCOLATE AND
MARSHMALLOW BALANCE OUT THE SHARP CRANBERRY FLAVOR,
CREATING A DESSERT FIT FOR ANY THANKFUL TABLE.

Vanilla or regular white chocolate

1 graham cracker, broken in half

1 marshmallow

Cranberry sauce (preferably homemade
. . . just because it tastes better)

Arrange the chocolate on half of the graham cracker and melt (see page 15). Roast the marshmallow. Once the chocolate has melted, remove graham cracker from heat and spread a spoonful of cranberry sauce evenly over the top. Add roasted marshmallow and remaining graham cracker.

candy cane

WHEN THE WEATHER OUTSIDE IS FRIGHTFUL, GATHER 'ROUND THE
FIREPLACE AND MAKE A CRUNCHY GOOEY DESSERT WITH THE EXTRA
CANDY CANES AND HANUKKAH GELT LYING AROUND.

Milk chocolate

1 graham cracker, broken in half

1 marshmallow

Candy cane pieces, loosely chopped

Arrange the chocolate on half of the graham cracker and melt (see page 15). Roast the marshmallow. Once the chocolate has melted, remove graham cracker from heat and lightly tap candy cane pieces in melted chocolate to secure. Add roasted marshmallow and top with remaining graham cracker.

gingerbread house

RESIST THE TEMPTATION TO SNACK ON YOUR GINGERBREAD HOUSE!
TRY THIS CHEWY GINGERBREAD S'MORE INSTEAD.

1 marshmallow

2 gingerbread cookies or slices
   of gingerbread

Assorted gumdrops

Roast the marshmallow. Once the marsh-mallow is roasted, spread it on one cookie or gingerbread slice. Wedge the gumdrops in the marshmallow and top with second cookie or gingerbread slice.

note: *Gingerbread is a strong flavor, so thinner cookies or bread slices are better for this s'more. If your bread or cookies are too thick, try using a graham cracker in place of the bottom cookie or gingerbread slice.*

chocolate liqueur cake

RING IN THE NEW YEAR WITH THIS ELEGANT OPEN-FACED S'MORE THAT COMBINES ANGEL FOOD CAKE, CHOCOLATE, AND BLACKBERRIES WITH THE SOPHISTICATED SWEETNESS OF WHITE CHOCOLATE LIQUEUR.

1 piece of angel food cake,
   around 1/2 inch thick
White chocolate liqueur
Nutella or melted chocolate
1 marshmallow
3 to 6 fresh blackberries

Cut angel food cake into a triangle or other creative shape, about the size of a graham cracker. Carefully pour white chocolate liqueur over angel food cake, allowing it to soak in evenly (you want the cake to be sufficiently flavored, but not soggy). Spread a layer of Nutella or melted chocolate on the cake. Roast the marshmallow. Once the marshmallow is ready, place it atop the chocolate layer, smashing it to cover the entire s'more. Top with blackberries. Eat as you celebrate!

resources

specialty chocolates

Some of the recipes in this book call for flavored chocolates not easily found in every candy aisle. This list of resources will help if you can't find your favorite flavor at your local specialty food store. You can also type in "specialty chocolate" or "chocolate" in any internet search engine for endless possibilities!

Dagoba Organic Chocolate
www.dagobachocolate.com
Chai, hazelnut, lavender, lime, etc.

Ritter Sport
www.eurofoodmart.net
Cornflake, marzipan, yogurt, coffee, etc.

Lindt
www.lindt.com
Coconut, orange, pear, pistachio, raspberry, toffee, etc.

Nutella
www.nutellausa.com
Hazelnut topping

Green & Black's Organic
www.greenandblacks.com
Vanilla white chocolate, mint, caramel, cherry, butterscotch, etc.

cookies

One of the best ways to spruce up a s'more is to replace the graham crackers with cookies. While some recipes call for specific, store-bought brands—such as Pim's biscuits and Stroopwafels—many others call for basics such as chocolate chip cookies, sugar cookies, and snickerdoodles. When making those s'mores, you can use homemade cookies, or purchase them at cookie shops or grocery stores. The key, wherever you get them, is to use soft, warm, chewy cookies in your s'mores. If the cookies you have aren't fresh and soft, heat them up on the grill or stovetop or pop them in the microwave. And if you do have time, make homemade!

LU Biscuits (Pim's)
www.lubiscuitsna.com
Pim's biscuits and other elegant European cookies

www.stroopwafelshop.com
Dutch wafer cookies

marshmallows

Add a specialty or gourmet marshmallow to your s'more for a new and tasty flavor combination.

www.plushpuffs.com
A huge variety of specialty marshmallow flavors

www.howthecookiecrumbles.com
Specialty marshmallow recipes and tips

Split Bean Coffee
www.splitbeancoffee.com
Specialty marshmallows, cookies, chocolates, coffees

index